Staff and Educational Devel   **ɪn**

Getting to Grips with Assessment

Sally Brown
University of Northumbria at Newcastle and
Brenda Smith
The Nottingham Trent University

SEDA Special No. 3
July 1997
ISBN 0 946815 59 3

Getting to Grips with Assessment

Contents

Chapter		Page

Introduction

The purpose of this publication is to help new and inexperienced lecturers who are tackling assessment, perhaps for the first time, to develop your thinking on assessment, reflect on your practice, make modifications where appropriate and to read more fully around the issue of assessment. Good assessment improves students' learning and helps the development of life-long learning skills.

If you want to make assessment an integrated part of the learning process, you need to look at a wide range of issues and questions, many of which we provide here. We believe assessment is a major influence on what students learn, how we teach, how students organise their studies and how individuals are able to progress in the future. As David Boud suggests:

> "Students can escape bad teaching; they can't avoid bad assessment." (Boud 1994)

Why Might We Want to Radically Review the Way We Assess?

Good assessment of students' knowledge, skills and abilities is absolutely crucial to the process of learning. Everyone concerned needs to have faith in a system, which must therefore be just, even-handed, appropriate and manageable. We believe that if we get the processes and practice of assessment right, then learning of the appropriate type will ensue. Boud again suggests:

> 'Assessment methods and requirements probably have a greater influence on how and what students learn than any other single factor. This influence may well be of greater importance than the impact of teaching materials." (Boud 1995)

In this paper we argue that the conventional ways by which we choose how to assess our students are just not good enough to achieve what we want, so we need to radically review our assessment strategies to cope with changing conditions we have to face in Higher Education internationally.

Influences on Assessment

Major changes have resulted from the introduction of modularisation or unitisation or curriculum delivery into institutions. This has often resulted in a whole range of problems such as unequal demands on students time, over-assessment, reduced time available for teaching, 'cantonisation' of the curriculum, increased workloads, more complex assessment regulations and so on.

At the same time, increasing student numbers have made traditional forms of assessment seem less appropriate, as the numbers of assignments handed in increases, the proportion of time necessary for assessing work grows and the pressure on staff to give meaningful feedback in a relatively short amount of time develops.

We are also seeing a greater diversity of students presenting themselves in our classes, with non-traditional entrance qualifications, varied backgrounds, unequal prior knowledge and experience and different learning styles.

Alongside this, many lecturers are becoming aware that a very wide range of methods exists, many of which are under-used, either due to ignorance or fear about their use. As we focus more and more on the key generic skills that constitute the 'graduateness' of a graduate, many academics are coming to perceive the need for different types of assessment. These will need to be able to test a whole range of skills and abilities which will be useful to students in their studying and in their working lives in addition to testing the traditional knowledge base we expect our graduates to possess. Assessment of these skills is an integral part of competence-based assessment programmes.

A further stimulus to improving our assessment practices is provided in the UK by the Quality Assurance Agency's guidelines on the assessment of the quality of educational provision in our institutions of Higher Education. The Assessors Handbook for the English system requires those who visit subject departments to evaluate:

- the use of assessment as a learning aid as well as a means of judging performance.

- the quality of feedback to students.

- the match of methods of assessment to the intended learning outcomes.

- appropriateness to the student profile, level and mode of study

- student understanding of assessment methods and criteria. (HEFCE 1996)

These appear to us to be eminently sensible guidelines, and lecturers in UK universities are usually keen to satisfy such requirements. At the same time, lecturers old and new often have intrinsic reasons to improve assessment practices, evidenced by their desire to find innovatory approaches to promote more effective learning.

In this paper we provide a set of principles we believe underpin best assessment practice,some important assessment issues, a series of questions your students are likely to ask you, so that you can think in advance about how you will answer them, a glossary of some less familiar assessment methods, some advice on how to choose the best methods by which to assess your students, some suggestions on how to streamline assessment practices to help you cope with heavy workloads and a list of references and further reading in case you would like to delve more deeply into the whole issue of assessment.

Chapter 1: Assessment by Principle

It is important when deciding on the best strategies for assessing students to base your decisions on sound and strategic thinking.The following section is based on the work of the Assessment group of the Open Learning Foundation, which collaboratively devised a set of twelve principles of assessment that we expand and develop further here.

The Purposes of Assessment should be Clear

There are a large number of purposes for which you might wish to assess your students. These might include to:

- provide feedback to students so they can learn from mistakes and build on achievements.
- classify or grade student achievement.
- enable students to correct errors and remedy deficiencies.
- motivate students and focus their sense of achievement.
- consolidate student learning.
- help students to apply abstract principles to practical contexts.
- estimate students potential to progress to other levels or courses.
- guide selection or option choice.
- give us feedback on how effective we are being at promoting learning.
- provide statistics for internal and external agencies.
- indicate standards and provide performance indicators.

Some less worthy (but just as powerful) reasons might include because:

- we've always done it.
- we have no choice, it's all part of the system.
- it gives us security.
- it makes us look busy.
- students expect it and make our lives miserable if we don't.
- we can hide behind it.

When we are planning to assess students, we need to be really clear about what the particular reason or reasons on this occasion are so we can design assessment instruments accordingly. We need to be able to justify, to students, our colleagues, moderators, external/professional bodies and ourselves why we have made these choices. Some further questions we can ask ourselves include:

- how well do our choices fit in with learning outcomes?
- who benefits from the assessment process on this occasion?
- are our purposes compatible with other aspects of the learning programme?
- do our choices fit in with local departmental/school/route requirement as well as those of the university?

Assessment Should Be Formulated as an Integral Part of the Case Design Process

Assessment should not be an afterthought. When planning or reviewing learning programmes, we need to ensure that the assessment is a key part of the discussions. A good starting point is to ask what we want students to be able to do, know and achieve by the end of the learning process. These will help us design our learning outcomes. Then we can design assessment tasks to match them.

However, we don't necessarily need one assignment for each outcome: assessment tasks can be synoptic, bringing together a number of learning outcomes in one assessment instrument. In each case, the decisions we make will have implications for learning, which is why their design must be fully incorporated in curriculum planning, and agreed by all those involved in delivering the programme.

Relevant Assessment Criteria need to be Identified and Used

These criteria need to be:

- linked to the learning outcomes.
- understandable by all the people who use them including the staff doing the marking and the students who receive the marks.
- clearly expressed, using language that is accessible, rather than jargon.
- explicit about what is expected from the students. This means that staff and students will have a good idea of the scope and extent of the work required, without this being over-specific.
- at the right level. Normally we should be able to expect the criteria for a particular outcome to become progressively more taxing as the student progresses through the learning programme. Therefore, towards the end of a programme the criteria used, for example, for a presentation should not be identical with those used earlier on.

At a university and national level in the UK, there is much debate about 'threshold standards' which determine to varying degrees how much we can specify exactly what we can expect students to achieve in each discipline, not only in terms of generic key skills but also in terms of subject knowledge. This is a thorny area which has much work yet to be done on it. (HEQC 1997).

We would also argue that student involvement in the **formulation and negotiation** of criteria helps them to learn effectively, enables them to make good judgments about their own progress and also makes assignment a really meaningful process.

Assessment needs to be Transparent

In order to have confidence in the system, all parties concerned (students, tutors, moderators, external examiners, employers, quality reviewers, professional bodies and others) need to understand the system and be assured that it is well-planned, works in practice and is regulated appropriately.

In practice this will involve:

- telling the students well in advance what is expected of them.

- providing a clear brief with indicators of what does and does not constitute satisfactory performance.
- giving indicators of what weight individual elements will carry.
- providing clear deadlines for handing work in.
- offering equivalent levels of support to students prior to submission.
- indicating how failure is communicated and can be redeemed.
- providing access to assessment regulations and information.

This can be achieved to some extent by:

- giving students a programme handbook (paper-based or virtual) at the start of the term/semester/ programme.
- providing information via the WWW.
- having in place good computer networked communication systems e.g. e-mail.
- providing opportunities to ask questions and have them answered

Assessment Processes need to be Consistent

All stakeholders need to know that:

- work marked by different tutors will be assessed to the same standard.
- individual tutors will assess work consistently, whether it is the first or last piece of work they mark.
- students will be briefed consistently, getting the same level of detail of information and the same ability to ask about criteria and outcomes.
- university systems are in place to moderate marking, whether this includes double marking, sampling or cross-moderation.
- administration of assessment will be consistently undertaken.

Some ways in which consistency can be improved are to:

- assess using published, agreed, discussed criteria.
- use marking schemes, proformas, model answers and marking protocols. (Brown, Rust, Gibbs 1994, p. 10 - 13).
- train new assessors how to apply local understanding of levels and grades.
- hold meetings of all assessors at which standards are compared.
- discuss 'borderline' and problematic cases before finally assigning marks.
- agree broad band marking systems to avoid arguments over one or two marks.
- agree locally or at an institutional level to what extent the whole range of marks will be used. (Some disciplines never award higher than mid 70%).
- use statistics from one year/ cohort /module /tutor to the next to compare results and look for inconsistencies.This will enable informed discussion of standards to take place.
- make effective use of external examiners to evaluate students within and across programmes and institutions.

- disseminate to all assessors the regulations which are being applied.
- consider implementing anonymous marking for written assignments to avoid accusations of bias in terms of gender and race.N.B. This is much more difficult to ensure in oral or live asscssmcnts where it is impractical to disguise identity.

Assessment Tasks need to be Valid

Assessment instruments and processes must assess what they set out to assess rather than what is easy to assess. This is often more difficult than it seems. Race (1993) says, tongue in cheek, "If you can assess it, it probably isn't it." If, for example, we want to assess the key skill of getting students working together in teams, we need to ensure that the task involves teamwork, rather than just writing about it. In addition, far too often, we assess a relatively small proportion of what we actually claim to deliver in a set of learning outcomes or an indicative syllabus. We often do this using a very limited range of assessment methods. (see chapter four).

We also need to ensure that the approach is valid. So, for example, if we claim to be assessing process as well as product, then the assessment instrument should be involved in assessing how the outcome was achieved as well as the outcome (report, presentation, etc.) itself. This is likely to require students to become involved in self assessment and peer assessment, as tutors cannot always find access to process.

Assessment should be Free of Bias

At all levels, assessment should offer students an unbiased opportunity to be treated equally and fairly alongside the students. This means in practice:

- adhering to criteria and not 'fudging' then when outcomes don't seem to fit your pre-judgments.
- ensuring that material on which assessment is based doesn't privilege particular groups in terms of ethnicity, gender, physical ability, sexual orientation, age, social class, ability to pay and any other means by which students can be discriminated against.
- students should as far as possible not be identifiable in written work by the 'foreignness' of their name or any other indicator.
- institutions, departments and teams should have in place systems for regulating and moderating assessment processes.
- facilities and practices should make it possible for all students to complete tasks on an equivalent basis.
- assessment methods as far as possible should be varied. Students who find it difficult to write at speed, work in the visual dimension, speak in public, pay for their own materials, should not be always either advantaged or disadvantaged.
- equivalent support needs to be given to students by tutors, technicians and information support staff. There should be no favouritism.

Assessment Tasks need to be Practicable

It is important to ensure that the tasks set can be achieved in the time available and with the existing constraints. These might include the facilities available to students, the accommodation used for activities, individual study and groupwork, the number of students who are all clamouring to use the same lab equipment, I.T. facilities and books and the amount of staff support available.

It is also important to check that the work being asked is at the right level for students at that particular stage in their programme. It can be problematic when students are being asked to undertake work which doesn't stretch them and which is not realistically achievable by students so early on in the programme and in the time available. Student performance is often substantially enhanced when they have the time and space to rehearse that on which they will later be assessed. Opportunities to learn from feedback at a mark-free and stress-free occasion often make complex tasks more achievable ultimately. We also need to take note of what other demands on students time are being made by our colleagues on other modules or parts of the course.

Assessment Workloads need to be Realistic

One of the major problems both new and experienced lecturers complain about is the amount of assessment that needs doing with increasingly large groups of students. Students also complain about workloads. When in the UK the quality of curriculum provision is assessed by HEFCE and others, a key issue is whether assessment workloads are manageable.

Some facts that contribute to effective assessment management include:

- staggered deadlines so everything isn't bundled together for students and staff. This also makes it more possible for students to get feedback on assessed work at times when they can use it to improve other pieces of work on the course.
- coordinated assessment timetables. This is not always easy under modular programmes, but uncoordinated assessment deadlines adversely affect student learning and cost academics dearly in terms of stress.
- assessment schedules published in advance. These enable both staff and students to plan their work more effectively.
- use of a range of means to streamline assessment.(see chapter six)
- administrative systems to support assessment. These can include having assessment clerks to receive and issue assignments, issue receipts for work, chase non-submissions, produce mark lists and so on. It is also important that the best available technology is used to provide a marks system that works.
- recognition by academic managers that assessment is an integral part of an academics workload. Too often lecturers are expected to get assessments done alongside all their other tasks with no recognition of the time and effort needed to plan, co-ordinate, assess and moderate marking.

Assessment needs to include a Wide Range of Methods

Most assessment in universities usually uses a really narrow range of methods, primarily traditional unseen written exams, essays and reports.If we want assessment instruments to be fit for the purpose for which they are designed, we need to select the assessment methods that best suit the task.

We might wish to diversify assessment methods because:

- some methods are better than others for each of the purposes for assessment we have identified.
- different methods advantage and disadvantage different students differentially.
- we need a wider range of methods if we are to assess product and process.
- we need a variety of methods to promote effective learning in different contexts.
- diversity prevents tutor and student boredom.

A range of less familiar assessment methods available to us is described in chapter four of this paper. We also need to consider what approaches we need to use when assessing. These include:

- **self assessment,** which involves students in the "processes of determining what is good work in any given situation" Boud 1995 and can help students to become more effective learners as they build up personal evaluative skills.
- **peer assessment,** by which students are involved in assessing other students, providing feedback opportunities for their colleagues and the development of comparative evaluative facilities for themselves.
- **group-based assessment,** which helps students to develop transferable interpersonal skills and may help to save staff time.
- **approaches involving negotiated learning programmes**, particularly through learning contracts by which students can negotiate how they progress through the stages of entry profile, needs analysis, action planning, tasks and evaluation according to their own needs and prior experience so that they can ultimately demonstrate that they have achieved the required learning outcomes.
- **computer-based assessment,** wherein, for example, students can get rapid feedback on their keyed in responses to your questions, with screens full of text giving them reasons why their answers were right or wrong.
- **work-place based assessment** by supervisors or line-managers for part-timers or students on placement, who are usually best-placed to assess student achievement in off-campus locations.

Assessment needs to Provide Feedback to Support the Learning Process

Students get really demotivated if they get no information about how they are doing. Tutors would usually like to give plenty of feedback but often feel themselves very hard pressed when dealing with the work of large numbers of students. Feedback is nevertheless enormously influential on student learning and can be very motivating or demotivating, depending on its nature, scope and means of delivery.

Guidelines on Giving Feedback

In order to make feedback a truly developmental process, you can:

- give comments back to students quickly while it still has a chance to do some good.
- find positive elements to comment on first and at the finish if at all possible.
- give feedback in as much detail as time permits.
- rather than carping, try to frame negative feedback in ways that directs the student towards improvement.

- criticise the work not the person.
- where possible, give reasons and explanations for your comments.
- give feedback on general issues to the whole group not just individuals.
- where appropriate and possible, give students an idea how they are doing as a whole within a learning programme, not just on this individual piece of work.
- avoid 'final language' (Boud,1994) which brooks no argument. If work is described as 'appalling' or brilliant' there's no where much to go after that developmentally.
- give plenty of advice on how the work could have been improved. Even excellent work can normally be enhanced by further reading, for example.
- direct students to facilities or resources to improve aspects on which they have been given feedback. These can be people, texts, packages, software, WWW sites and other students.
- ensure that feedback relates directly and primarily to the assessment criteria.
- consider collecting examples of good and bad work with your feedback comments and publish them with the permission of the students involved.
- where possible provide in class opportunities for comparison and discussion of feedback in a supportive and developmental environment.
- make sure students can make sense of your feedback, avoiding illegible writing, impenetrable codes and meaningless notations e.g. question marks.
- avoid discussing students by covering their work with masses of red ink and crosses.
- consider using instantaneous feedback, for example, computer based tests, in class feedback sessions and so on. For more information on this, see Brown, Race and Smith (1996).

Assessment needs to be Integral to Quality Assurance Procedures

Effective assessment is absolutely fundamental to the process of student learning and therefore the assessment of the quality of educational provision of any university must make examining assessment core to the process.

This can be assured by:

- making sure assessment is properly considered in the validation and review process, with none of the difficult issues ducked.
- giving responsibility to every member of staff who assesses to monitor their practices. Student views are an important part of this process.
- making sure everyone knows who has ultimate responsibility for the quality of their assessment instruments and processes.
- ensuring that, as part of the annual review process, time is made available to review aspects of assessment and look at ways to improve it by drawing up an action plan with deadlines and duties for named people.
- involving the external examiner in the assurance of students within and across institutions, and taking notice of and acting on their suggestions and recommendations.
- making full use of central administrative support to provide statistics and to distribute and collate information about assessment practices.

Putting Principles Into Practice

To enable you to reflect on how well you are currently doing with assessment, you might like to try filling in the table below.

Good Assessment Practice

Criteria	Rating of current practice	Possible improvements
Integral part of course design		
Relevant criteria identified & used		
Transparent		
Consistent		
Valid		

Criteria	Rating of current practice	Possible improvements
Free of bias		
Tasks that are practicable		
Realistic workloads		
A wide range of methods		
Provides feedback to support learning		
Integral part of quality assurance procedures		

Scoring: 0 = completely fails to meet criterion; 1 = meets this criterion to a small degree;
2 = broadly meets this criterion;   3 = fully meets this criterion .

Chapter 2: Assessment Issues.

The next session is designed to pose a number of questions for you to consider when designing assessment instruments, having taken account of your earlier deliberations. This section raises issues, first discussed by Gibbs (1989) and developed by us further here and provides an agenda for discussion.

Is The Assessment Summative or Formative?

Assessment is often described as being either one or the other, formative or summative. These are often presented as opposites , whereas they are really ends of the same continuum. However, while formative assessment is primarily characterised by being continuous, involving mainly words and with the prime purpose of helping students improve, summative assessment instead tends to be end point, largely numerical and concerned mainly with making evaluative judgments. A pre-submission critique of work in progress is a typical example of formative assessment, whereas an end of programme exam exemplifies summative assessment.

Inevitably, no form of assessment is purely summative or formative. For example a final year exam result gives students realistic feedback about their likelihood of getting funding for a higher degree and formative feedback usually contains language of judgment ("good", "lacking in depth", "untidy", "inadequately referenced", "exceptionally detailed" etc.). It is important to provide for your students an appropriate balance of both.

Is The Focus on Continuous Assessment or Final Exams?

To rely solely on final assessment misses developmental opportunities for learning from feedback. If assessment is to be integral to student learning, it seems sensible to integrate it fully in the process. Where the only assessment for a unit or module is a final exam, it is a good idea to look for ways of incorporating formative assessment throughout the programme of study where feasible. This might include in-class quizzes, self or peer assessment and computer-based assessment to increase the amount of formative feedback without providing excessive additional loads on tutors.

Is It Process or Product You Are Trying To Assess?

Sometimes, for example, we are equally interested in the groupwork that leads up to the production of a presentation as the presentation itself. Assessment that only focused on the end product would therefore be inadequate. In designing a fashion garment or in undertaking chemical experimentation, the steps that led up to the final design, including the mistakes and designs rejected, can also be important in helping to make a realistic evaluation of the activity. The assessment instruments you design should take this into account.

To What Extent Is The Assessment Formal?

In the past, judgements have sometimes been made about student performance during informal occasions such as. social events, field work, coffee break discussions and so on. Any such personal evaluation normally should not influence assessment decisions unless they provide evidence of performance against clear and explicitly stated criteria and unless all students have equivalent opportunities to demonstrate their abilities.

How Much Independence Does The University Have in Setting Assessment Tasks?

Many professional bodies are extremely directive in the ways in which assessment is designed and conducted. They may influence, for example, the type and scope of questions set, the marks which constitute satisfactory performance and the level of performance expected. In some cases, the papers are all externally set and marked. Here individual lecturers have no flexibility in designing summative assignments to stimulate learning. Assessment decisions here tend to be more constrained than when the responsibility for assessment design remains within the university.

Are We Aiming Towards Convergent or Divergent Assessment?

When setting questions and tasks, we need to be clear whether we want all students to end up with the same or similar outcomes or whether we want them to have divergent outcomes, with opportunities for individual choice. Our decisions may be influenced by availability of resources (so we don't get all the students chasing the same text), by worries about plagiarism (it's harder to cheat if your answer is not the same as your neighbours), according to how much we want to promote creativity (this may be highly motivating) and how much time and energy we can devote to assessment design.

Computer-based assessment can, for example, be divergent when an individual student is presented with a unique set of questions from a large question bank. Where all students answer the same multi-choice questions, chances to cheat are higher.

If we want students to follow their own interests, we can enable them to choose and formulate their own topics within agreed framework. Learning contracts (see chapter four) are another means by which students can be offered opportunities for divergent assessment.

What Kind of Referencing Are We Using?

Norm referencing means looking at a cohort of students as a whole and deciding where in rank order an individual student comes. With large cohorts of students, it is possible to expect results to fall within a normal bell-shaped distribution curve, with few at the extremities getting very high or very low marks and most banding around the middle.

Criterion referencing is where students are judged against a predetermined set of criteria, and if everything is satisfied, they get 100%. Frequently, if a criterion is not satisfied, students can have further opportunities to try to achieve the standard. It is therefore not sensible to try to fit results from such systems into a normal distribution curve.

When decisions are made about degree classifications, sometimes competence-based formulas by which students achieve set criteria are used as a basis for norm-referenced decisions, despite the fact that these measures (first, 2i, 2ii, etc.) tell us very little about individual students' competence.

Rarely in Higher Education students are measured against their own previous performance, in terms of the value added to their competence, knowledge and skills at entry. This is also known as progression or **ipsative referencing.**

Some argue that norm referencing can be unfair as it depends on the cohort against which individuals are being judged, and this is not a fixed standard. Others argue that criterion referencing makes life too easy for students, as it makes it possible for large numbers to get top marks. Ipsative referencing is seen as valuable in terms of formative feedback, but not so helpful and describing summative outcomes

Whichever referencing system is used, it must be used consistently and not expected to match the expectations of any other system.

Is The Focus Diagnosis or Prediction?

Using a medical metaphor, we need to decide whether we are looking at a student's current status and deciding what must be done to remediate or improve it that is providing a diagnosis, or are we trying to make a prediction of likely outcomes, for example, will a given student be better to the French or Spanish option on a combined course, so as to suggest particular courses of action. Either way, we can then guide our students and help them make informed choices.

Are We Assessing What Students Know or What They Have Learned?

This is an important but difficult distinction. Gibbs (1989 op cit.) describes an Open University research study of students on a Science foundation course, where two groups of students, one who had taken the course, and one who had not, achieved not dissimilar scores in an exam. This seems to indicate that it is extremely difficult to measure how much learning gain students have achieved, so progression is extremely difficult to measure. For this reason, measures of added value are complex to design and use. However we still need to think about how this can be achieved, so many lecturers like to develop ways of eliciting baseline data against which they can measure learning.

Is The Focus on Content Specific or Generic Skills and Knowledge?

Increasingly in higher education we value students' abilities in key skills as much as their subject knowledge. Employers tell us they want graduates who can work collaboratively, retrieve information, solve problems and communicate effectively and we also recognise that students often learn more effectively when they are proficient in these skills. We need to decide how important each of these areas is in designing assessment instrument, and to attain a balance that is appropriate to specific contexts and levels.

Chapter 3: Difficult Questions Your Students May Ask You

This section is designed to help you prepare for the questions that students are likely to ask you about the assessment process. You cannot possibly be expected to know the answers to all of these, but we suggest you go through the list, marking the one you feel are most likely to be asked in your own particular context. Finding out the answers to these prioritised questions from colleagues, mentors, managers and the published regulations will help you feel confident you can cope with students' assessment queries.

When will I get my mark for this assignment?
Does the department / university have a policy on the maximum time students have to wait for assignment return?
Are all marks unconfirmed until ratified by your exam board?.

What will happen to my examination papers?
Are they returned to me? If so when?
How long are they archived?
Are they shredded eventually?
Do I get any feedback on individual questions?
Can I see my marked paper?

What happens if I wish to appeal against my mark?
Can I challenge the academic judgment of the marks?
Will I be penalised for questioning the system?
What do I do if I feel I am being victimised?
Where can I find the written details of approach procedures?
What if I think marks have been added up wrongly?
What if I feel I have been treated unfairly compared to my colleagues?
What if I feel that the tutor who marked me was harder than the tutor who marked my friend for the same assignment?

Why do lecturers always ask for assignments for different modules at the same time?
Can I get any chance to balance my workload?
Do they know what is going on for us?
Will they ever listen to our pleas?

What happens if for good reasons I can't sit the exam or get my work in on time?
Who do I talk to?
What are the procedures?
How lenient are they?
Can I be sure everyone is treated equally on extensions?

What can I do if I think the assignments are biased towards certain groups?
Can I argue that all the case study materials are focused on male (or female) interests?
Can I make a case that all the materials are really insular in that they never mention issues that affect my

experiences from the country I come from?

Can I argue that everything is based round a lecturer's own narrow point of view?

As a dyslexic student, what help can I expect?

Will I get longer to answer exam questions?

Can I take a dictionary / laptop in with me?

Is there a policy which clarifies procedures?

Will I be penalised for my spelling?

Can I expect the tutor to check my coursework pre-submission?

Will I be given a chance to choose the topics on which I do assignments?

Are we given tight guidelines about the topic?

Is it very prescriptive?

Can I follow my own interests?

Are we to be given opportunities to be creative?

Am I given any chances to learn from my mistakes?

Can I resubmit if I've got a low (but not fail) mark?

Will I get any feedback before final submission?

Do I get any second chances?

Will I be told what criteria I am being assessed on?

What do I do if I don't understand them?

Who can I talk to? How much tutor time can I expect?

What do I do if no criteria are available?

Can I challenge the criteria if I think they are inappropriate?

Do all the tutors use the same criteria for the same assignment?

What can I expect in the way of feedback?

Will I just get a mark or can I expect detailed comments?

What can I do if I want more feedback?

Is there a university policy on this?

Am I entitled to time to discuss my assignments / exams with the tutors?

Will I be given advice on how to make my work better?

Can I expect this in writing?

If I disagree politically or philosophically with my tutor, will I get worse marks?

Are there any systems by which I can ask for another marker?

Who can I ask about this?

How can I be sure I will be treated fairly?

What do I do if I can't afford the materials I need to undertake the assignment?

Are there any materials available free?

Will allowances be made if my work is hampered by shortage of materials?

What will I do if my printer goes down just before I am due to hand in an assignment?
Will I be given extra time?
Can facilities be made available to me?
What if it's the university's equipment that's at fault?

What happens if my coursework is stolen or lost by me or my tutor?
Can I be given credit for marked work that I can't subsequently produce for the moderator?
What happens if I dispute with my tutor whether the work has ever been handed in?
Will I get a receipt for my handed-in work?

How secure and accurate is the university's mark recording system?
Is data entered accurately?
Can people hack in and change my marks?
What can I do if I think something has gone badly wrong?

Does all my work have to be word processed?
Will I get a worse mark just because I don't have my own computer?
What happens if I haven't got good IT skills?
Does the university provide support to help me learn keyboard skills?

What proportion of marks are given for presentation?
How important is spelling and punctuation?
What if my graphic skills aren't very good?
Will my dissertation have to be bound?
Do I have to pay for this?

Will allowances be made if English isn't my first language?
Will I be given any help reading and checking for accuracy?
Does the university provide support?
How many marks will be deducted for my English?

Is any support given to students with special needs?
What if I can't sit comfortably for two hours in an exam?
Are special arrangements made so I can see / hear properly in oral assessments?
If I need food or medication, can I leave the exam room?

Will I be assessed orally?
What happens if I hate speaking in public?
Can I ask for a substitute assessment?
What if I have specific special needs?

Do I have to be assessed as a member of a group?
What if I don't get on with the others?
Will we get the same mark?
What do I do if a group member doesn't contribute equally?

When I am taught in mixed groups from different years of the course, or from different modes of delivery (e.g. part-time/full-time), will I be assessed in exactly the same way?
Are the same criteria used?
Can I be confident that the system is fair?
Will any special allowances be made for anyone?

Will part-time, franchise and off-campus students get the same access to university services, materials and staff to support their learning and assessment as full time students do?
What do I do if I think I'm being unfairly treated?
Can I take short loan or set text books home?
Are any special arrangements made for us/

How much help can I get from other students?
If I like working with a partner/ colleague /friend, will we be accused of cheating?
What if we both agree on a lot of things?
What if we use identical reference sources?
What happens if we both independently get the same answer?

What do I do if I think someone has copied my work?
Who can I talk to?
How can I prove it was mine originally?

To what extent can I use material I've got from the internet?
Do I have to say where I got it from?
Does it matter if I don't really know?
How do I check that what I gain on the internet is accurate?

How many copies of my work do I need to make?
What if I can't afford the photocopying?
Is it my responsibility always to keep a copy for security?

What do I do if I just can't cope with the workload?
Who do I talk to?
Can I get any support?
What do I do if I feel I'm cracking up?

What will happen if I have a disaster?
Is there any compensation if I am really ill / a family member dies / my child is sick/ my car breaks down, I have to go to the dentist etc.?

What do I do if I feel my tutor is harassing me and offers assessment advantages in return?
Is there a university policy?
Who can I turn to for advice?
What is my legal position?

Will my work be double marked by two separate tutors?

Do they get to see what each other has written or will it be blind marked?

How do they make sure that they are marking consistently?

What if one give me a really high mark and one gives me a low one?

Will the tutors know whose work is being marked by them?

Will it have my name on it or just a number?

How can I be sure I won't be victimised/

Will I be asked to mark my own and other students work?

How will I know what to do?

What safeguards are there?

Will it be fair?

What do I do if I don't agree with the marks?

A Word of Advice

This is not a comprehensive list of everything you may be asked, but you shouldn't be daunted by it either. These are often the questions that experienced lecturers have difficulty in answering too. They are provided here to start you thinking and to prepare you so you don't get caught on the hop by questions to which you can fairly readily find an answer.

Chapter 4: Glossary of Some Less Familiar Assessment Methods.

Throughout this paper we have suggested the use of a wide range of assessment methods beyond the more traditional time-constrained unseen exams, reports and essays. Here we provide very brief descriptions of some of the more unusual assessment methods in the hope that it will stimulate you to find out some more about them, consider if any are appropriate for your particular purposes and contexts and perhaps to try them out.

Annotated Bibliographies. Students are required to produce a list of texts and information sources on specified or agreed topics to an agreed referencing convention. They then annotate these with a commentary which includes evaluation of what they have read.

Articles. Students can be asked to write on set or agreed topics to an agreed length with a timescale, for a specific audience,eg. a journal, magazine or newspaper. This can be equally or more taxing than a traditional essay, but can be easier to mark.

Book Reviews. Students are required to write short (300-500 word) accounts of designated or chosen books, articles and other texts. These usually include an evaluative element and demonstrate depth of reading and level of understanding in concise formats.

Case Studies. Scenarios can be provided giving realistic details of contexts upon which are based questions and problems for students to answer. Often case studies are provided in advance of a time-constrained assessment.

Critical Incident Accounts. Students working on placement or in practice can keep diaries, journals or logs in which they record their experiences. From these, they can be asked to select one or more critical incidents and write about the context, what happened, what were the outcomes, how the theoretical material they learned in the course underpinned the process, how they would do things differently now and any further reflections.

Essay Plans. Instead of writing a full essay, students can be asked to produce a number of essay plans which demonstrate their preparation, planning and reading on a set or agreed topic. They can be particularly useful to demonstrate breadth of reading and thinking, and to provoke formative feedback.

In-tray Exercises. Students are provided with a dossier of papers to read and prioritise initially and then work on, with a variety of tasks and new information given at intervals through the exam. These simulate real practice where unknown elements and irrelevancies are often encountered.

Learning Contacts. Normally students and tutors negotiate a programme of learning which includes an **entry profile** indicating the level of achievement at the beginning, a **needs analysis** in which what is to be learned is agreed, an **action plan** of how the learning is to be undertaken and means of **evaluation**, so it is known what has been achieved. Frequently a learning contract will go through this cycle on a number of occasions during a programme of learning. It is important that clear criteria for achievement are agreed.

Learning Matcrials. Students can be asked to prepare a learning package, perhaps for sixth formers or younger children, on a specified or agreed topic, using perhaps audio / video tapes, pictures, graphs, tables, photos and material on computer disks as well as text. This can require them to cover complex material in accessible formats and tests a range of skills as well as specific subject knowledge.

Logs. These are lists of activities and outcomes that students check off during a period of learning. For example, some sandwich students have to indicate perhaps 200 competencies that they have practised on a number of occasions to a specific level during a year's placement.

Multiple Choice Questions. often computer-based, MCQs provide easy to mark assessments in which students select or enter responses to questions. The best provide instant feedback on right and wrong responses, contributing to student learning. The best packages require a level of skill and knowledge in answering questions that was not thought feasible previously.

Open Book Exams. These provide students with the chance to use any or specified resources to support the writing of answers to set questions in time-constrained contexts. This can reduce stress for students and removes over-reliance on memory and recall.

OSCEs (Objective, Structured Clinical Examinations). Often used in medicine and associated professions, OSCEs comprise a number of testing stations around which students progress, typically being tested on ten or more learning outcomes for about 10 minutes each using live patients, simulations, lab tests and so on to assess a wide range of skills and knowledge.

Portfolios. Portfolios exist in many forms. Most are centred on the provision of evidence by students for the satisfaction of specified or agreed learning outcomes in a structured format, often including a reflective commentary. They can include a range of media such as audio and video tapes, computer discs and artifacts as well as text of all kinds.

Posters. Individuals or groups can be asked to present the outcomes of a period of research and / or preparation in visual form. This is often an A1 poster including text and images. The criteria for assessment need careful clarification in advance. Peers can often assess the posters alongside tutors, using tick sheets containing the criteria. This provides a chance for students to see and learn from each other's work.

Question Banks. Students can be assessed on their ability to produce perhaps one hundred questions on a topic. The first few will be relatively easy to formulate, but the task becomes progressively more demanding and taxing. This can help students to recognise what they do and do not know about a topic.

Reflective diaries. In these, students are asked to record their learning or other experiences over a period of time, interspersing narrative with a reflective commentary that includes their reactions and thoughts about what has happened. These sometimes lead directly to action plans.

Seen Exams. The question to be answered in a time-constrained context are provided in advance, enabling focussed preparation. These can prevent stress and mean students don't 'question spot' or panic.

Short Answer Questions. These are used in exams and tests to ensure wide coverage of materials. Students write brief answers to a large number of usually compulsory questions. Nowadays software is being developed to enable short answers to be optically recognised when inputted on a keyboard, thus making short-answer questions easier to mark.

Simulations. Text- or computer-based realistic environments are provided for students who then demonstrate flexibly their ability to answer questions, resolve problems, show competence, perform tasks and take actions according to changing circumstances within (normally) a set time frame.

Here we have given only the sketchiest details of the methods to give a flavour of what is involved. More details and other methods can be found in Brown & Knight (1994) chapters six and seven.

Chapter 5: Choosing the Most Appropriate Methods of Assessment

Having considered a wide range of methods, it is important to decide when to use any particular method individually or in combination. More than 80% of assessment in UK universities comprises essays, reports, and traditional time-constrained exams. Assessment that is 'fit for purpose' uses the best method of assessment appropriate to the context, the students, the level, the subject and the institution. To help you choose the most appropriate methods, here are some questions to stimulate your thinking. These are adapted from a section in **500 tips on Assessment** (Sally Brown, Phil Race and Brenda Smith) 1996.

1. If you want a written assessment instrument, which of the following should you choose from? Consider the best uses of essays, reports, reviews, summaries, dissertations, theses, annotated bibliographies, case studies, journal articles, presentations and exams.

2. Should the method be time-constrained? Exams, phase-tests and in class activities might well be the most appropriate for the occasion. Time constrained tests put students under pressure, but are usually fairly good at preventing cheating.

3. Is it important that the method you choose includes co-operative activity? If it is important, you might choose to assess students in groups, perhaps on group projects, poster displays, or presentations.

4. Is a visual component important? When it is, you might choose portfolios, poster displays, 'critique' sessions or exhibitions.

5. Is it important that students use information technology? When this is the case, computer-based assessments may be best, either getting students to answer multiple-choice questions, or write their own programmes, or prepare databases, or write information stacks for hypertext, or material for use in CD-ROM systems or on the Internet.

6. Do you wish to try to assess innovation or creativity? Some assessment methods that allow students to demonstrate these include: performances, exhibitions, poster displays, presentations, projects, student-led assessed seminars, simulations and games.

7. Do you want to encourage students to develop oral skills? If so, you might choose to assess vivas, presentations, recorded elements of audio and video tapes made by students, assessed discussions or seminars, interviews or simulations.

8. Do you want to assess the ways in which students interact together? You might then assess negotiations, debates, role plays, interviews, selection panels, and case studies.

9. Is the assessment of learning done away from the institution important? For example, you may wish to assess learning done in the work place, in professional contexts or on field courses. You may choose to assess logs, reflective journals, field studies, case studies or portfolios.

10. Is your aim to establish what students are able to do already? Then you could try diagnostic tests (paper-based or technology-based), profiles, records of achievement, portfolios and vivas.

Chapter 6: Streamlining Assessment

Most of us would like to find ways in which to make the process of assessment less arduous, freeing our time for other things. While recognising that assessment is a fundamental means by which we support student learning, the following menu of ideas is proposed to help reduce some of the drudgery of marking written work. Some will be well-suited to specific contexts, others will not. Select any that seem helpful to you!

Use an assignment return sheet. Find out if these are available in your department or devise one yourself. Typically, an assignment return sheet includes boxes for student identification (name and number), tutor identification and the assessment criteria as set out in the assignment brief. Tutors then fill in boxes with brief comments, tick boxes and/or circle grades on a Likkert scale to give an indication of the means by which the mark was achieved.

Assignment return sheets are a widely-used method of providing fast feedback to students and may be supplemented by additional lengthier comments on scripts if required and permitted. For an example, see Brown, Rust and Gibbs (1994) p. 40-41.

Get the students to fill in assignment return sheets themselves. You can then also fill one in (without looking at theirs) and then compare their own evaluation with yours. Further comments can then be given especially where students' views of their work markedly differ from yours.

Try statement banks. These make use of the fact that most of us use a number of comments repeatedly when writing on students work. These comprise 'statement banks' in our heads that we can use in a number of ways.

1. **List the comments you make regularly, type them up, number them, issue them to students on a photocopied sheet.** Then you can put the relevant number on a script alongside the text to which it applies, saving you writing the same points out endlessly.

2. **As you mark a set of scripts, list your comments on an OHT.** Number them and put numbers in student's work as above. On the next occasion on which you work with the whole cohort, you can show them the OHT, invite them to compare their scripts with your comments on screen, and note what you have said. In this way, students are required to spend some time taking comments on board, you save some writing time and people who have made mistakes know they are not alone.

3. **List the statements on computer and use a package to extract the items you want from an individual student.** Clever software will enable you to provide individual passages of continuous prose commentary for each student relatively easily. Many High School report systems in the UK use this process. Not everyone likes computer-generated prose, but it can save time.

Use model answers. Provide students with a worked example, where appropriate, so they can compare their assessment products with the model. Feedback on individual answers can then be minimal and can relate to specific areas of the model answer.

Use an assignment report. Give students numerical marks only, but supplement them with a lengthier report handout for the whole group that tells them how many attempted each question, what the average, maximum and minimum marks were, what constituted a good performance and so on. Add into this more specific comments, examples of good and bad answers, common errors and omissions and so on, so students get an overview of their performance.

Use I.T. to support assessment. Investigate the uses of computer-based Multiple Choice Questions as part of a mixed diet of assessment. Don't feel you have to write all the MCQs yourself (they are easy to write but hard to write well!). Find out what is available for sale, who else in your discipline is using them, who might give or swap you question banks (US publishers commonly provide MCQs to accompany textbooks when these are recommended texts on a course, for example).

Involve students in their own and each others assessment. This will not necessarily save a lot of time as it needs careful organisation at the front end of the process to ensure that students mark to criteria and check whether evidence of achievement is demonstrated. Self and peer assessment also provide extra opportunities for formative feedback, particularly at interim stages. With rehearsal and training, students can be involved not only in marking to agreed correct answers, but also making quite sophisticated evaluative decisions when appropriately supported. (Brown and Dove 1990)

Consider giving feedback only on selected aspects of students' work. Where students have a number of assignments, you could perhaps concentrate your feedback on one or two areas on each assignment, perhaps information retrieval and data analysis on one, ability to argue cogently and present work well on another and so on.

Think about word limits. Often we set fairly arbitrary word limits for students assignments, without thinking this through clearly. Length does not equate with depth or breadth! When we ask for 5,000 words, it is worth considering whether 4,000 would do. When we ask for 2,000 word essays, might we not consider using some of the shorter format methods described in chapter four to assess the same kinds of outcomes?

Find out whether administrative help is available. Some universities provide admin. support to collect in work, make up mark lists, follow up non-submissions and so on. This can save you lots of time.

It is not suggested that these ideas will answer all your problems, but used in combination, judiciously, selectively and from time to time you may find they make your life easier!

Chapter 7: An Assessment Manifesto

In this paper, we have argued for assessment systems that are designed to fit the purposes for which they are needed. We conclude with a manifesto which embodies the values which underpin our suggestions. You might like to consider the extent to which these items underpin your own assessment practice.

Those who assess student work need to ensure that assessment practices can:

- enable individual differences between students to be celebrated rather than be regarded as problematic, and be accommodated in ways that ensure equivalence if not identicality of experience.

- provide a measure of choice for students within the assessment process.

- clearly explain the purposes of the assessment to all stakeholders so that the process is open, transparent and sound.

- provide students with meaningful and useful feedback that can help them to enhance their performance and learn at a deep level by reflecting on their performance.

- provide our institutions with the data they require, in meaningful formats, on time, so that students can be awarded degrees, certificates and other awards as the outcome of their studies.

- be an integral part of curriculum design, so that meaningful choices can be made.

- involve criteria that are clear, explicit and public, so that students and staff know what constitute threshold and higher standards for achievement.

- be of an appropriate amount to be manageable for staff and students, without stretching either group beyond the bounds of reason.

- be demonstrably valid, reliable and consistent.

- be open to periodic review and reflection leading into quality improvements.

The choices we make in our assessment practice are instrumental in determining whether assessment is genuinely a part of the learning process or whether it becomes an increasingly meaningless and bureaucratic task, which exhausts and frustrates all parties. The challenge remains for us all in our own institutions to ensure that assessment becomes a truly dynamic and educational process.

References and Other Useful Reading

Boud D (1994) Unpublished keynote speech at SEDA conference.

Boud D (1995) *Enhancing Learning through Self Assessment,* London: Kogan Page.

Brown G, Bull J and Pendlebury M (1997) *Assessing student learning in Higher Education,* London: Routledge.

Brown S and Dove P (eds) (1990). *Self and Peer Assessment,* Birmingham: SEDA.

Brown S and Baume D (1992) *Learning Contracts - a theoretical approach,* Birmingham: SEDA.

Brown S and Baume D (1992) *Learning Contracts - some practical examples,* Birmingham: SEDA.

Brown S and Knight P (1994) *Assessing Learners in Higher Education,* London: Kogan Page.

Brown S, Race P and Rust C (1995) 'Using and experiencing assessment' in *Assessment for Learning in Higher Education,* ed Peter Knight, London: Kogan Page.

Brown S, Race P and Smith B (1996) *500 tips on Assessment,* London: Kogan Page.

Brown S, Rust C and Gibbs G (1994) *Strategies for Diversifying assessment in Higher Education,* Oxford: OCSD.

Gibbs G (1989) *Module 3 Assessment for the Certificate in Teaching in Higher Education by Open Learning,* Oxford: OCSD.

Gibbs G, Habeshaw S and Habeshaw T (1991) *53 Interesting Ways to assess your students,* Bristol: TES.

Gibbs G, Jenkins A and Wisker G (1992) *Assessing More Students.* No. 4 in the Teaching More Students series, London: PCFC.

Gibbs G (ed) (1995) *Improving student learning through assessment and evaluation,* Oxford: OCSD.

Harris D and Bell C (1990) *Evaluating and Assessing for Learning,* London: Kogan Page.

HEFCE (The Higher Education Funding Council) (1996) *The Assessors Handbook,* London: HEFCE.

HEQC (1997) (The Higher Education Quality Council) *Assessment in Higher Education and the Role of Graduates,* London: HEQC.

Knight P (ed) (1995) *Assessment for Learning in Higher Education,* London: Kogan Page.

McDowell L (1995) 'The impact of innovative assessment on student learning' in *Innovations in Education and Training International,* Vol. 32, Number 4, November 1995.

McDowell L (1986) Enabling Student Learning through Innovative Assessment' in *Enabling Student Learning: Systems and Strategies,* Wisker G and Brown S (Eds), London: Kogan Page.

Open Learning Foundation Assessment Issues group (1995) *Workshop Materials,* London: Open Learning Foundation.

Race P (1995) The art of assessing' in *The New Academic,* Vol. 4, Number 3, Autumn 1995.

Rowntree D (1989) *Assessing students - How shall we know them,* London: Kogan Page.

Stephenson J and Laycock M (1993) *Using Learning Contracts in Higher Education,* London: Kogan Page.